An Open Mind

Jacquelyn Schultz

Presentation by *BookLeaf Publishing*

Web: www.bookleafpub.com

E-mail: info@bookleafpub.com

ISBN: 9789357744027

First edition 2023

Fragile

I am a porcelain doll
Not meant to be played with
Like my soul, I am fragile
Said the eyes of the daredevil

Mirrored

It is your eyes in the mirror
As if you are right here or
Your hair color
Showing right over
Our almond-shaped eyes

I Still Need You

I stood there
Near the bottom stair
Staring out the window
Little do the kids know
My lungs could barely breathe
Motherhood has a chokehold on me
Tears streaming down my face
I so badly wanted out of this place

But I needed you
I needed you to see me, to be with me
I needed you to listen when I spoke,
I needed you but you left me broke
On the fact that you said you didn't want me
How you acted in the past is beyond me

But I needed you
I needed you to hold my hand and say
everything is alright
When I had my child at night
Instead you chose to abandon your oldest
When I needed you, your heart was the coldest

I still need you
Even when I found my strength inside
Day by day my inner child has died
She needs you to hold her close
She always needed you the most

I still need you
To hold me in your arms
I need you to hold me and look at the stars
Can we forget the generational trauma
I am tired of you being gone, Mama

It Controls Us

Clear cognizance of
The entity amid time
Is nonexistent

Brother

With the bond we share
And how much I care
Our lives, like no other
We are sister and brother

Now we find each other in foreign worlds
All of our childhood troubles we hurtled
Together, side by side, bonded by souls
In the moment where life now takes a toll
I have the urge to give you a call
But I would rather have you down the hall

When we were kids, we would talk all night
Reassured each other everything was alright
I could go to bed calm and at ease
Knowing that I had you near me

You were my first best friend
A hand willing to lend
Someone to play with and pick on
We grew together but now we've moved on

You are always in my heart
Regardless of our distance apart

The bond we share
Will always be there
A special bond like no other
We are sister and brother

Grounded

A step onto the green grass, tickling my bare
skin
A breath I take as I close my eyes, while closing
out the world
Earth's green energy arising from my feet,
throughout my legs
Unraveling its empowerment
Entering the heart of my soul
Fulfilling my arms and neck
Earth's energy reaching my crown
Connecting my entire soul with nature's beings
Vibrational energy radiating around me
Tall like the trees
Warm as the summer sun
Content as the leaves drifting in the breeze
Grounded, my inner self finally reaching peace
A moment alone in nature is a moment to live

The Rising

The euphoria
Sparkling from my aura
Rids aporia

A February Day

Grey skies soothe the mind
Bringing me peace at this time
Snowflakes blanketing the ground
Branches from the tallest trees faintly sound
Chilled air filled with silence
Erasing my thoughts of mental violence

Waiting for the sun's rays to show and shine
I release my breath with the hopes to find
My inner child content and at peace
Finally healing as the struggles release
The sun's warmth grows on my face
One step at a time, I grow at my own pace

The Eye

One time I held a human's eye
A different kind of thrill and high
Once in a lifetime moment
I was honored, a bestowment
In my hand laid a human's eye

The Room

The room
Answers are found
The dead show the living
Evidence lets justice proceed
Autopsy suite

A Saturday Morning

A small yellow flickering flame
In the dark quiescence of an early morning
Snowflakes melting onto the window frame
Anticipation builds while my espresso is pouring

The beginning of a new day
Giving me the chance
To admire my plants on display
All shades of green, together they dance

I Am

In my heart, I am a rainbow
I have days where I feel black, although
I choose to raise above the darkness
Bringing myself to a higher consciousness

I radiate the energy I want to receive
My soul chose this body, I believe
I must trust the Universe
I shall always put myself first

The Offspring

When I hold you my soul feels white
My soul is magnetic with yours
Contentment, safety, it feels right

When I hold you the rest of the world disappears
Us together, side by side
Just stillness and breathing, my dear

When I hold you I have no worries
Your soft skin and little hands
I lose all my insecurities

When I hold you, I become plentiful
You smile and say, "I love you"
It enriches my heart and soul

A Rose

A rose
Soft and silky
Shimmering in the sun
Vibrant, bold, standing tall and strong
Growing prickles and thorns for protection
Sweet fragrance idles in the air
Swaying as the wind blows
A perennial
A rose

Day of Birth

The day of my birth
Was a day of purpose and surprise
I know what I am worth
I am my own franchise

I can build an empire
To create the world I want to live in
I must follow what I desire
While using the talents I've been given

Heaven

Yellows, oranges, and pinks paint the sky
Levitating in a basket woven of wicker
All my problems suddenly die
A moment of floating in Heaven
Nothing else matters but this moment
When I entered a new halcyon zen

Your Cards

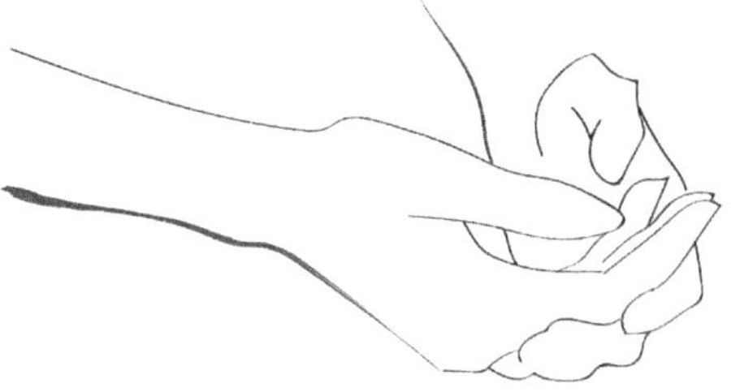

I understand now, that I am older
It was not your choice
To be dealt the cards
You are just the holder

My Mind

This is my own human existence
I recognize I need to outdistance
Myself from the mad world
That has my mind swirled
And focus on my own consciousness

* 9 7 8 9 3 5 7 7 4 4 0 2 7 *